Just Jack Russells

Just Jack Russells

Photographs by Dušan Smetana
Text by Steve Smith

WILLOW CREEK PRESS

MINOCQUA, WISCONSIN

For Jess and Nicole, Milo and Molly
—S.S.

Just Jack Russells
Copyright © 2001 Willow Creek Press
Text © Steve Smith
Photographs © Dušan Smetana

Published by Willow Creek Press
P.O. Box 147, Minocqua, Wisconsin 54548

Art Director: Pat Linder
Editor: Andrea Donner
Production Design: RSK Book Design

For information on other Willow Creek Press titles,
call 1-800-850-9453

Printed in Canada

Library of Congress Cataloging-in-Publication Data
Smith, Steve, 1947-
  Just Jack Russells / text by Steve Smith ; photography by
Dušan Smetana.
        p. cm.
  ISBN 1-57223-212-9 (hardcover : alk. paper)
  1. Jack Russell terrier. 2. Jack Russell terrier – Pictorial works.
  3. Photography of dogs. I. Title.
    SF429.J27 S65 2001
    636.755–dc21   2001003686

Contents

"If you eliminate smoking and gambling, you will be amazed to find that almost all an Englishman's pleasures can be, and mostly are, shared by his dog."

—George Bernard Shaw

Introduction

Mr. Shaw may not have had the Reverend John Russell of Devon, England, in mind when he crafted those lines, because it's doubtful the good reverend, flamboyant though he was said to be, took much stock in smoking and gambling. But if you take out that part, then the passage would fit John — Jack — Russell like a glove.

What Parson Russell, the Vicar of Swimbridge, liked to do was hunt foxes, and terriers were not only part of the equation back in the mid-1800s, they were one of his personal weaknesses. But he wasn't quite satisfied with what was available to him in those days. Until, through the force of sheer luck, he came upon Trump, the dog that would become the wellspring of the Jack Russell terrier. Using Trump as the basis of his brood stock, the good Reverend set about going after the traits he wanted. What emerged was a dog that shifted away from the fox terriers of the day — and remains so — one capable of going into a fox den and flushing the little rascal out or holding it at bay underground until the Parson showed up. The dog was also able to keep up with the hounds and the horses, and was, at least to the Reverend's eye, just the right blend of tenacity, enthusiasm, courage, and speed.

Exactly how this came about has, like the history of all such early dog breedings, been lost in the mists of time. But what the Parson eventually got was not a fox terrier; it was something unique, named for a rather unique individual.

Though common reference is to the dog as a breed, the JRT of today is technically a strain, not a purebred. That's because this new terrier's evolution didn't stop with Parson Russell's death, and over the years breeding has been done primarily to ensure the dog's hunting heritage — the drive — and not for a universally accepted appearance. When behavior and achievement are the goals rather than conformation, those folks doing the breeding have a tendency to try a pinch of this and a smidge of that, contributing their own ideas about what physical requirements are needed for a good hunting dog. In other words, the breedings were less standardized and often experimental.

A funny thing happens to a dog breed when this route is taken. One breeder's idea of what should be added is different than another's. There are inbreedings, linebreedings, and outcrosses. As a result, you have what breeders like to refer to as a "broad genetic background." The other thing that happens is that when a pair of Jacks are mated, the resulting pups can't be completely, accurately predicted because there are all those genes floating around in there, so the dog does not breed "true to type," and breeding true to type is one of the things that defines a purebred dog. Or a purebred anything.

So today, there are long-legged and short-legged JRT's with smooth coats, rough coats, and broken coats. This is not to imply that there are no standards or that Jacks are mutts — far from it. In fact, there are devotees of each type that have formed a variety of organizations, each dedicated to their ideal JRT: the Jack Russell Terrier Club of America, the Jack Russell Terrier Association of America, the English Jack Russell Club of America, and the Jack Russell

Terrier Club of Great Britain, and others. They have their own registries and standards and resist cross-registrations. In short, these folks are about as dedicated and feisty as their dogs. But they all have the good of the dog in mind and we can assume that someday their differences will be settled . . . or not.

What breeding for hunting with Jacks has done, regardless of conformation, is to fix a drive and personality in them that seems to be uniform. These are hunting dogs. They have been bred for hunting, they will hunt constantly if given the opportunity, and practically all their behaviors can be traced to the hunting drive. In the world of the canines, the Jack's single-mindedness for the hunt approaches the level of weapons-grade plutonium.

That's what this book celebrates — this dog's delightful way of looking at the world.

Steve Smith
Traverse City, Michigan

PORTRAITS

The eyes are the
window to the hole

Jacks are terriers, which comes from *terra*, as in terra firma. They are earth dogs, chase, corner, get down in the hole, and root 'em out dogs. As a pure hunting breed that "goes to ground," these dogs are constantly on the alert for the chance to do just that very thing. In fact, "alert" could be the single best term to describe them. You can see it in their eyes.

Sometimes, for the uninitiated, it's tough to tell a Jack without a program — the coat, the coloration, the size and shape can vary from type to type. What does not vary are the eyes, eyes that often look past the here and now to the middle distance, the eyes that sparkle with imagination and, too often, mischief.

Nothing gets past the gaze of a Jack. The German shepherd down the block at 100 yards or a spider at point-blank range—all come under the same intense scrutiny of the eyes that dance with an intelligence that is astonishing. There are those who say the Jack Russell is the smartest dog in the world. Perhaps, but there's no question that it is among the most focused.

LIVING WITH
JACK RUSSELLS

Born to be riled

Whoever it was who coined the cliche, "They're not for everyone" had to have Jacks in mind. Living with a Jack Russell terrier is an experience, but it is not difficult if you know the rules: Rule One — Jacks love adventure; Rule Two — Jacks love to have fun; Rule Three — in case of any misunderstandings, refer to Rules One and Two.

Despite their reputation for what often seems to be hyperactivity, Jack Russells are kind and loving family dogs. They dislike being separated from their people, their streak of independence notwithstanding. The happiest Jack Russell owners are the ones who understand that they are not owners — they're partners. However, the dog must know his place in the pack as one of the sub-dominant members. You must always retain the upper hand. If not, you'll wish you had.

Owing to their heritage of going down and under, Jacks enjoy close quarters. A backpack or something that would seem to be too confining for such an active dog feels natural. Where another breed of dog may enjoy sleeping on the foot of your bed, a Jack would much prefer being at the foot of the bed — but under the covers.

The perfect relationships between Jacks and their people result when the human partners are as active as the dogs. This is a go-along dog. Forget a kennel or a life outside. That's for other, lesser dogs. The Jack's life is one where the humans understand that these are insistent animals. They will insist that they be included and, as most Jack people know, if you disappoint them, they have their ways of letting you know about it.

These dogs — if we refer to the Rule of Adventure — have the same need to see something new as an intelligent child. In order to properly socialize these dogs when they are young, the wise owner exposes them to a wide variety of experiences. And being adaptable — one major measure of intelligence — the dogs adjust. And thrive.

Of course, Jack Russell people themselves tend to tilt a few millimeters off from the typical pet owner. Rarely do you see the sort of dedication to a breed these folks exhibit. Spending time with, caring for, laughing at, and trying to outwit these dogs is something of a full-time occupation. And those who have accepted and revel in the challenge have a way of announcing it to the world.

Moments of calm are rare, and so memorable. Normally, a snapshot of a Jack Russell's world must be taken with a fast shutter speed, especially when they launch one of their patented warp-speed tears though the house and over the furniture. It can make for interesting conversation if the new neighbors happen to be visiting.

ids and Jacks are a whole other subject. While they are loving and good around children, the typical Jack Russell terrier will not allow itself to be hamhandled with impunity. Unintended abuse by a child who does not understand these dogs can result in trouble. Kids under the age of six or seven have to be watched closely. And if they are someone else's kids, the owner must be as alert and operate under the principle that everyone knows a lawyer these days. These dogs aren't mean; far from it. They just don't suffer fools gladly.

J acks can be cocky, arrogant, willful, and stubborn, intent upon getting their own way. They are easily bored, so living with them is often an exercise in patience with their ways. It is also one of life's more amusing experiences because these dogs are, above all else, characters.

An often-heard description — coined by those who love the dog the most —
is "Jack Russell terrorist". . .

. . . and they have been described with some degree of accuracy as "a thug in clown's clothing." If a dog can swagger, Jacks swagger.

Jack Russells are territorial animals. They have their domain, a well-defined home range, like all the *Canids*. And within it, they know everything that's going on.

Apparently lacking an internal sense of proportion — or maybe a gyroscope — this is a small dog that doesn't know it's small. A Jack doesn't try to intimidate the big dog next door with bravado — he actually thinks he can whip him because he really believes he's bigger. Another truism we can attach to Jacks: It isn't the size of the dog in the fight, it's the size of the fight in the dog. But only to a point. Unfortunately, Death by Rottweiler is all too common for these wonderful animals. But peaceful coexistence and friendship with another dog in the family is the rule rather than the exception. On the other hand, cats, birds, and hamsters in the same house are not such a good idea.

PLAYING HARD

O, give me a home
where the terriers roam

The apparent idyllic apartment life of "Eddie" — aka "Moose" — on the television program *Frazier* notwithstanding, Jacks don't do well in condos, small yards, or in the city — at least not as well as they do with room to rumble about and race and terrorize the local small mammal population and assorted unauthorized varmints. This is a dog of the countryside. That's how and where he was bred, and it is what he remains. Often possessed of a short attention span, an underemployed Jack will figure out a way to keep himself amused. And if he does, the chances are, you won't be. They don't intend to be destructive; they're just looking for a little diversion.

This is triple-distilled, muzzle-velocity, concentrated, industrial-strength dog. When he or she is on a mission, there is nothing shy, demure, or retiring about them.

nd talk about energy! There are springs in those legs. But all such play has its genesis in the drive to hunt. Leaping for a toy is the determination to catch and grapple and hold. A game of tug-of-war is the relentlessness that makes them so single-minded in the pursuit of their quarry. The curiosity and the antics that make us laugh are based in the need to hunt and explore, the intelligence honed to outwit the witty.

E ven a bounding tennis ball, to the dog's genes, is probably a prey that is escaping, triggering the instinct to chase and catch and conquer. On the other hand, it just may be a tennis ball and the whole enterprise looks like fun. And Jacks are addicted to fun.

Stalking, chasing, tussling, exploring, that wonderful imagination and intelligence are never stilled. This is what Jacks are about. It is why play is their work and work is their play; it is why the dancer becomes the dance.

WORKING HARD

Go for it!

ompetition. This is where it gets serious. The athletic nature of Jack Russell terriers has quite naturally led to competitions among them to see who is the best of the best. The events are: agility, conformation, go to ground, obedience, racing, trailing, and to a lesser extent, high-jumping. Major meets around the country attract the best dogs, and by these champions, the gene pool is enriched, because those that win are in demand as breeding stock.

The human competitors must wonder what happened. They vaguely remember thinking that a Jack Russell would make a nice pet; the next thing they know, the family car has been traded for a truck, all available vacation time is spent crisscrossing the country to competitions, and a wing has been added on to the house to hold all the impedimenta required for training. And there's probably dog hair in the wine glasses. The competition bug has bitten.

These canine athletes make us proud. That's the reward, after all: pride. And eighty-five cents worth of blue ribbon. Naturally, we can't compete with only one dog, and multiple events call for multiple dogs. And there has to be a farm team with young prospects being developed. This is serious business carried out in an atmosphere of friendliness and cooperation. The satisfaction seems to grow with a life of its own.

The focused competitors have ways of announcing where their hearts and minds are. The rest of the world — careers and day-to-day living — are distractions to be dealt with between terrier trials.

The competition village that springs up at each trial brings together friends and competitors, and friendly competitors. They watch the dogs, note who's coming on and who is past prime. They discuss breeding and training, and all things JRT.

At first, the dogs act a little baffled by it all. It seems like a lot of commotion for a little running and jumping and crawling around in the ground. But the seasoned dogs soon realize that the competing and winning thing is right up their alley, and they come to know the difference between practice and game day.

And even though there isn't an official event, there is the quasi-sanctioned matter of who has the most unique and imaginative Jack Russell stuff. Sometimes, as much effort goes into this as into the events. It's all part of the wonderful Jack Russell culture.

onformation shows are won by those who have bred to a standard, which depends upon which JRT organization the competitor belongs to. Each believes their dogs represent the best the breed has to offer.

Agility competitions take a combination of training and performance in order to win. The dog must know what to do, be able to instantly follow commands, and do it under pressure and with precision, because the dog with the fewest errors wins — in case of a tie, the win goes to the fastest. This event, like all of them, takes time and dedication.

Racing is what these dogs perhaps love to do the most. Get from Point A to Point B as fast as possible. The need for speed. Chase the lure, hit the hole in the straw first, get a ribbon and a treat back at the truck and your ears scratched — what a life!

At the end of the day, and at the end of a career, a Jack Russell competitive athlete can be proud. To win is not as important as to try. And in retirement, there is plenty of time to relive the glory days.

PUPPIES

Hold on to your heart

The insightful young writer Jonah Goldberg once commented: "Every generation, Western civilization is invaded by barbarians; we call them 'children.'" Well, Jonah could have just as easily made that "puppies." A puppy is a package of potential — a friend, a protector, a confidante, a clown — and someday nothing but a bittersweet memory. In between, there is a lot of world to be explored.

There is very little more endearing than the dedication that canines have for the task of motherhood. One of those little spotted squirmers that seems so helpless will someday be digging up the tulip bulbs because he or she thought you looked like you could use a little help.

In the canine world, the bigger they are, the sooner they fall. It's a rare Great Dane that sees ten years, and a Labrador retriever at twelve is ancient. Jack Russell terriers can still be thinking up amusing things to do at fifteen. And they don't slow down much, either.

J ack Russells enter this world as undisciplined as yahoos — and some leave it about the same because they didn't get what they needed: even-handed and consistent discipline. These are testing dogs, and they are not intended for those who lack the fortitude it takes to hold them to the mark. As canines, they will fill a dominance vacuum if they perceive it exists. If they see you as the Alpha pack member, they — and you — are happier.

The number of Jacks up for adoption with rescue organizations attests to the fact that some prospective owners thought they could change nature. These dogs are delightful animals, but they are, as stated earlier, not for everyone. They are high-octane, high-maintenance guys and gals who demand your attention. The best advice is not to bring one into your family unless you have the time, the space, and the temperament for the job. But if you do, you'll find what thousands of others around the world have found: There is no better companion, no more intelligent crony, and no more lovable clown than the Jack Russell terrier.

For Additional Information:
Jack Russell Terrier Club of America, Inc.
P.O. Box 4527
Lutherville, MD 21094-4527
Phone: (410) 561-3655
Fax: (410) 560-2563

The Jack Russell Terrier Association of America
(formerly the Jack Russell Breeders' Association)
PO Box 115
Winchester Center, CT 06094
(203)379-3282